ARVYDAS DAŠKUS

**The Practice of Karma**

# KINGBOOK

CONTENT:

ENLIGHTENMENT

AURA

CANCER

LANGUAGE OF CREATOR

PERFECT STATE OF EXISTENCE

DEPRESSION

SPECTRAL RESONANCE OF CROWN

ESCAPE COVID-19

VILNIUS

2020

This KINGBOOK is alive. It contains tools to change the flow of your life to a positive one. You will find the biggest challenges are inside of your soul. In the deepest gaze – Creator's ocean. And the method of direct communication with Him is just here. Let us read, learn, and use this opportunity to become clairvoyants, find safety in boundaries of dangerous life and avoid Covid-19, depression, cancer as well as teach others. This book is meant for all of those who are on a path towards spiritual development. It is an amalgamation of personal experiences and knowledge, which came into being through analyzing and contemplating complicated life experience of the author. The author expects these analytical guidelines to be of value to their readers. Everything presented here is meant to be used individually. This comes only from a realm of personal destiny practices. If, upon using the provided information, a reader decides to seek healing, they cannot replace conventional medical treatment. All people who try to use the tools presented here themselves, should only do so in parallel with traditional medical methods prescribed to them. Following the instructions of your physician is essential.

The main purpose of this book is to share the information collected and plant the seeds of knowledge that might assist in applying these ideas and methods in practice. Everyone who chooses to follow these guidelines shall start on a safe and well-trodden path towards a harmonious connection with the Origin of Life, the Creator-God inside all of us, who generates the flow of life, lives in the center of our essence, protects us.

# ENLIGHTENMENT

Monday, 18 February 2019, 9:29 a.m. Just a few minutes ago I sent the manuscript of my book that I was working on for almost forty years, to the BMK publishing house. In an e-mail, I informed the BMK representative about a possibility to start working on the layout of a book, called *"Practice of Karma. The End to the Era of Cancer?"* The text of the book was attached to the e-mail. This meant the end of relentless work and a huge personal relief for me. The thought that the process of deliberating, discovering, editing and revising, which lasted for almost forty years, has finally ended was hard to comprehend. Of course, I knew that the text will require some additional corrections, but the most important ideas have been formulated and the sometimes-agonizing search for the truth has finally come to an end. As the book has become a vessel of my entire experience, I sensed a strong desire to process and really feel the entirety of what I have achieved. So, I went to my living room, made myself comfortable on the sofa and started thinking. Suddenly, a wave of very unusual feelings came over me.

The room changed. Even though it seemed the same, the surroundings started to become gradually brighter and gained a certain glow. Looking at every little piece of the walls, windows and furniture gave indescribable satisfaction, and it almost seemed I was becoming one with everything I witnessed around me. All of a sudden, I noticed that the room was shining. Everything – the walls, furniture, paintings, flowers, numerous figurines on the shelves – seemed to have come to life, emitting unearthly, delight-filled light. Eventually, that feeling started dominating everything around, and suddenly a feeling of unbelievable and soul-crushing nirvana came over me like a huge wave in an ocean. I became a part of that wonderful feeling and melted into it, even though remained flawlessly conscious at the same time. Suddenly, it struck me as lightning over a dark city – I was experiencing ENLIGHTENMENT. This discovery brought extreme excitement, as I understood that this is a blessing sent to me by God. And I received it as a reward for everything that I had achieved, suffered through, collected bit by bit from my own experience, transformed into conclusions, theses, assumptions and finally handed over to my readers. At the same time, it became a lifeline to many people drowning in various catastrophic situations. To those, who were trapped inside the prison of cancer. The moment had a strong relation to the ideas set in the book. First of all, with the idea that one must find ways to directly communicate with the origin of life – the Spirit or the Creator-God inside all of us. Immediately, a thought crossed my mind, plunging me into an unbelievable revelation: the phenomenon that was happening right there and then was the Creator's response to my desire to learn methods of direct communication with Him, expressed in the book! He supported the idea of direct communication! These thoughts merged with the constantly flowing feeling of the marvelous tidal wave of nirvana. There were moments, when it became so intense, I almost disappeared entirely, disintegrating in the waves, having only one ability – to feel that bliss in every inch of my body. During these flashes, I did not feel any desire to analyze or understand, as these were the moments of perfect fusion with the Creator. On the top of the mountain of knowledge, they left me with a feeling of bliss, similar to the joy a baby feels rocked in the strong arms of its Father. And these were perfect moments of liquescent love. As a wave subsided, my consciousness used to clear up, bringing the rational thinking back. All the thoughts that flew by were filled with heart-warming smiles. In the midst of this euphoria, I did not want to scream, cry or express my emotions in any other extreme methods. In the deeps of this state, I felt the heavenly peace of the Creator. A humble peaceful smile, brimming with absolute trust. During these moments of clarity, I started simultaneously observing internal, recognizable images from my past journeys and extreme experiences. I remembered the moments from my trip around America clearly, as if I could see myself from up above – crossing vast empty spaces in a tiny Ford at night. And I understood that nothing bad could have happened to me then, as I was constantly watched over by the same mysterious force bringing my memories back at this very moment. This revelation brought a big gratitude-filled smile to my lips. I remembered that I did not feel any fear nor anxiety wandering that enormous country, as at that time – just like during many other stages of my life – I was led forward and protected by the Creator's hand that brought me peace and filled be with trust. And the same hand was filling me with this incredible feeling of Enlightenment at this very moment. In the flow of destiny, nothing is isolated, everything merges into this one unbroken stream. In it, the positive path is marked by selflessness, honesty, subservience to the origin of the Spirit and the depth of one's Faith. In a way, all of us live in the Creator's palm, enveloped in his loving and protective gaze. Our Father is caring, and the power of His love knows no equals. We can only try to reciprocate everything He gives us. So, while the flow of these visions and experiences kept on going, the waves of the enlightenment nirvana continued to wash over me in the same slow rhythm. I was constantly either propelled unto the peak of total dissolution, or pulled backwards towards consciousness that enabled my analytical thinking. The fantastic glow of the room fascinated me. Even though all things and the walls remained the same color, they seemed much brighter and more vivid. Observing each detail filled my heart with pulsating joy. My blissful smile did not disappear for a second. Quick glances to my watch revealed that the blissful state I was in had been going on for a long time – almost two hours – but I did not have the slightest wish to stop that feeling or somehow end this extraordinary experience.

After some time, I heard the key turn in the front door. It was my wife.

Having taken her coat off, she came into the room and said in a surprised voice: "What happened? You look very strange."

"Yes," I replied, "something amazing is happening with me, I'm in state of enlightenment."

Little by little, the feeling started fading away. At the same time, I felt that I will be able to enter this state in the future as well. This brought me peace. Moreover, I understood that everything I had written in my book was truthful. Everything I had just experienced was a reward for my honest journey towards a new experience, for my discoveries that had built bridges towards the Truth of the Creator-God that I had understood, found and uncovered. For my unconditional subservience to Him. I could feel this in my heart almost physically, but instead of pain it was unprecedented excitement. I accepted everything as a gift and encouragement. This moment embodied everything worth living, enjoying and suffering for in this incredibly beautiful and challenging world of the Creator-God. I am so thankful for that.

## YEAR LATER

One year has passed by. Now I am able to review the impact my book *"The Practice of Karma. The End to the Era of Cancer?"* has made on its readers. The book has been received with huge interest, but the amount of people who were able to free themselves from cancer by using the techniques described therein has been minimal. Minimal, but not zero. At the same time, I have noticed that the society's interest in the book has been growing, especially in the testing technique described. For many, this represents the main obstacle of solving many seemingly unsolvable issues, also the problem of the cancer. The cognitive instrument described in the book raises doubts and questions to many. It is quite understandable, as getting to know something intangible that cannot be physically touched is an enormous challenge. However, for those who put enough effort and time into finding the subtle and mysterious vibration of the Spirit-sent signals and are able to recognize it as an answer to their question, the value of this gift is immeasurable. Nonetheless, at first, by analyzing the tasks posed by this publication step by step, I will try to concentrate on the main statements that have helped me make my final conclusions.

## HUMAN STRUCTURE

Humans and life itself have been created by a phenomenally limitless and powerful being, called the Creator-God. One of the components of the Creator's body is a subtle, structured substance of cold plasma that permeates all areas of living and non-living environment, controlled and managed by the Creator. Inside of all living beings (humans included), there is a sacred component of the Creator's body that creates life, controls behavior, protects and observes us – His children – from within. This segment is called the Spirit. This is a concentrated part of the Origin, Ancestry, Source or – applying a universally recognized concept – the Creator-God. Under His will, it is introduced into existence. In order for a person to be separated from the Creator and gain their own personal existence, the same Creator-God uses the given Spirit segment to form individuality, or the so-called Soul, by adding many different traits to it. In order for the Soul to gain experience, grow and develop, it is given an instrument – a human body. The most important part of the body, the brain – is a bridge or an intermediary. Only through the brain that the instrument of immaterial cognition, the mind acts in the material world. The mind not only performs the analytical function, but also connects all three basic parts of the human structure: The Spirit, the Soul and the Body. The mind enables a human being to consciously alter their internal conditions, by shifting their attention from the outside towards the internal fields of a human entity. Apart from structure, this complex spiritual-physical being, which we call "us", has quality as well. During our birth, we are given quality, untainted during the course of life, and it is always determined by the spiritual quality of the phenomenon that has created us, i.e. the Creator-God.

> After mentioning the Creator-God, I feel a need to stop and explain. I do not relate this name and His general activity in the biosphere and, more specifically, inside us, with any religious rhetoric. In the entire context of this publication, the Creator-God is a personally perceived phenomenon active inside of us. Only having chosen the subtle personal path of getting to know Him directly, can we understand Him and use His gifts. This statement corresponds to the teaching of Jesus, the son of the beloved Creator-God, found in the Bible. Actually, this is the same "path, truth and life" that opens the door to a personal relationship with the Father. I do understand that the teachings of Jesus reveal the idea that

the Faith is our Love for our Creator-God, which gifts us with amazing traits and gives meaning to any person's life. Due to this, the entire content of this book associatively serves the statements presented. This is how I perceive the revelation of the essence of the biggest church in the world – the internal spiritual origin of a human being – and the personal path towards getting to know the Creator-God. If, while on this path, a person is able to choose correct steps, it is probable that they will be rewarded with new incredible traits. They are the gifts from the Creator, ought to be used for the remainder of one's life.

The following should be accepted as a law: The Creator-God has not created any bad soul. During the course of life, the most important task of each human being is to treat your Soul in the right way and improve it constantly. Only the Soul that accomplishes the plan of the Creator-God and develops itself in a correct way can improve and become adequate to the quality of the Creator's body, also known as the Spirit. It is at this moment that the two origins become one, and, apart from the harmony of the divine Spirit, the Soul acquires immortality as well. There is a popular belief that the same human being is able to be born many times. This belief forms an integral part of many religious and philosophical teachings. Edgar Cayce, a phenomenal American clairvoyant, confirmed that reincarnation does, indeed, exist. However, one has to remember that a Soul that leaves this earth after having an imperfect life, is forced to undergo essential transformations after coming back. Souls, which have been unable to reach perfection, do return to life, but not before losing certain traits or acquiring new ones, i.e. they come back to this realm having the same basic Spirit, but being different. They are not the same persons anymore. The only way to stay who you are is to meet the Creator's expectations, develop the gifts that have been given to you, i.e. aptitudes and talents, and, by putting enough effort and creative drive to work, live your life in a way that implements His creative plan. To put it in simpler words, one has to become the Creator-God's friend and partner. Only by avoiding all the conflict created in the world by different religions, can a person become free in God's eyes. Only then can a person choose their own ways of bowing to the Creator-God, expressing their love and finding the right words to speak to Him. A human being has total freedom to choose when and where this should take place, as well as one of the existing sanctuaries for such actions. For the Creator-God, only one thing really matters – the sincerity of a person who tries to express themselves while speaking to Him, and their perception of the Creator-God as a loving Father that is everywhere around us, but especially inside of us. It is so extremely important for each and every one of us to look for paths into His heart through work, thoughts and feelings that the Creator likes. Such an intrinsic connection frees a person from their tedious routine, from certain labels, "scriptural interpreters", false prophets, the burden of guilt constantly preached by ideologists and the load of never-ending prayers. In the said realm, a person has a right to create their own personal forms of serving God, or, in other words, their personal religion. A religion that does not ignore, does not berate and does not seek to destroy any other existing form of religious expression. Personal religion can have numerous creative paths. It is a flow of feeling that is born in the field of human creation and expression, leading directly from a person's heart to the heart of the Creator-God. For some, it can be a stream of their personal verbal creation, for others – meditation in nature, filled with concentration and feeling one with the surroundings, for others – the state of focus and dissolution while painting and so on. Nonetheless, it does not close any doors to universally accepted religious practices, rituals and services using conventional methods of various religious communities. All human beings are free. I truly believe that Jesus wanted to create a community of free, non- dogmatic and non-fanatic people, and only saw phariseism as a negative phenomenon. Whereas, materialism, still prevalent in the scientific field and characterized by negating the existence of the Creator-God, is irreversibly disintegrating, and it is becoming quite obvious that the indicative methods to recognize the patterns of the Creator-God's activity will be detected soon, enabling the scientific and the mystical experiences of humanity to finally merge into one. It is wonderful that the image of aggressive materialism, that has been developed in the scientific fields for centuries, is gradually dissolving nowadays. I believe that contemporary science has come very close to finally identifying the phenomenon of Spirit inside of us. It is probable that the latter will be identified as the activity of a material informational core inside a human being in a state of cold plasma, and even more evidence will be gathered, proving that the latter is the force that generates life of a person. It is not difficult to take one more step further and acknowledge that He is the source of all life realization programs inside of us. But science is still not ready to understand – that this area is the medium, from which and through which the endless force of the Creator-God flows into us. It gives life to each and every one of us and enables the expression of all personal traits given to us by Him and the Creator-God's vision of our life, called Destiny or Karma. It is this specific space (pay attention), where one can find the codes of protection against fatal or karmic diseases. Having understood all of this, everyone can start their path of collecting spiritual experiences. Finally, following the

Creator-God's plan, all of us are provided with a possibility to consciously develop our creative capabilities and grow in the sacral field, in order to achieve a very specific goal – to move towards a phenomenon of internal changes, called miracles. Being on this path for many years, I have set a personal goal to myself to find a way – how to cure cancer?

## AURA

A person's aura comes from the radiation of a person's Spiritual center or the Creator-God inside of us. Soul and body are only intermediaries in this process. A developed aura, which can oftentimes be observed visually as well, typically manifests around people who have deep **faith**, or, in technical terms, around those who are extremely permeable to the radiation of the Spirit.

> This is characteristic to people of truth, whose Soul is close to the Spirit or the Creator-God inside of us, and who experience the Creator's love at a great extent and are able to reciprocate it.

I have been observing auras for quite some time now. Little by little, it has become a habit of mine, and I have been really surprised by the fact that many people I have met did not have the slightest idea of what aura is. Moreover, the idea that aura can be seen seemed even more outrageous to them. So, I started experimenting – after explaining the origin of auras, I offered simple explanations that could help them learn how to watch auras. Due to this, many previously oblivious people suddenly had many revelations. This and the teaching itself made me happy, especially when I noticed that these simple lessons were starting to change people's lives. It did not come as a surprise, though, as a person who is watching an aura can "visually touch" the real body of the

Creator-God and experience the direct impact of the Spirit or the Creator inside of us. This experience changes people, they start feeling elevated and oftentimes find themselves having creative capabilities they never knew they had. It is understandable why this subtle life-changing experience creates an intuitive desire to seek spiritual values later on. The previous formal religious belief, commonly perceived as "knowing about God", changes. It becomes an inner state, a real spiritual power. And this power inevitably makes one's life shine in a totally different light. All of this takes a form of a very gentle evolution. Drastic momentary changes do not appear. The Creator inside of us, or the Spirit, talks to a person in a cautious way, by suggesting individual paths towards cognition. There is no coercion in the Creator's language. Without demolishing previous belief system, this method of cognition simply improves them. A certain depth appears, due to which a person does not feel forced to change neither their common rituals of serving the Creator-God nor the methods of human communication in the society or family structures. Rather, the internal spiritual landscape expands, illuminating everything with deeper and brighter colors of direct cognition.

## CANCER

In this publication, I will try once again to dive deeper into an analysis of the subtlest gift offered to the reader – an ability to interpret the signals of the Spirit and use while learning how to overcome life's challenges and troubles. The principle that allows us to look at cancer through a new lens is simple – everything in life happens for a reason, and especially cancer arrives at a human body having a very specific cause. And the cause is not "eating too much carcinogens", as one might think. In order to understand that often very obscure reason, we must learn how to scan the flow of our life and detect that one fateful moment, when a fracture occurred, opening the doors for the disease. This simple scanning instrument, known since the times of pharaohs, is a pendulum (even simple ring on a string would suffice as well). Another factor that seems confusing to many readers is the simplicity of the method. The technique is so simple, it is almost humorous. The contrast is even more obvious due to enormous inertia of thinking. People are unable to think about cancer in simple terms, they do not know how to get away from the centuries-old and widely-acknowledged assertion, according to which cancer means **the end**. Well, if not the end, then at least stepping near the edge of an abyss. This situation takes away rational thinking and a possibility of calm analysis and makes people act desperately, i.e. they start erratically looking for a doctor, planning operations, chemotherapy, radiation sessions and so on. This is not bad, as it is usual and normal practice. When I started writing my book *"The Practice of Karma. The End to the Era of Cancer?"*, it became very clear that pushing a patient outside the boundaries of this type of thinking is unforgivable. New behavioral strategies can only be created if one does not try to inhibit the ordinary course of actions, and, instead, suggests only a parallel theoretical and practical program. These two methodologies do not contradict or confront one another. The principle of their coordination is quite simple: the more efficient one wins. So, what's next? I suggest going back to the possibilities of the radiosthesic instrument, the pendulum. This unique instrument has been appreciated since ancient times until this day, and people who are able to use it effectively are usually treated as visionaries in the society. In many realms of life, when complex tasks must be accomplished, the pendulum proves itself to be a trustworthy partner that is able to produce results in the situations where conventional methods do not work. However, to me, just like, I think, to many of you as well, this instrument seems a bit too capricious. Its language is often hard to interpret. Thus, my goal has been to simplify the testing technique and introduce something direct and organic, i.e. something that would put to work not only the vibrations felt in the fingers holding the pendulum but my entire SELF. Soon I understood that, in this case, the method of scanning with your palm, which I have been using for many years to treat patients, works perfectly fine. The simplicity and efficiency of this method can be better understood by using *"Radiosthesic Testing Field SHORE"*, a publication attached to the current book. At the bottom part of the field you can see a strip of the colored lines. They present all colors of aura. The importance of the task will undoubtedly help to prepare for the transformation and to enter a specific state of the test. The goal is to find the specific moment in your life, cancer started manifesting in your body. This strip on the testing field represents the entire course of your life up until the current moment. The task is to find the sole moment of a faithful mistake happened in your life. Just one on the strip – timeline of your life. The task has been simplified to bare minimum. All the lines on the strip represent the seven colors of an aura. If you start moving along the strip with pendulum, or waving along the strip with your palm, certainly you will feel vibration lightly resonating with the vibrations of your body. In addition, you will see on the picture of testing field my eyes and be followed by my intense gaze. This is the helping tool through which I will send towards you an impulse of psychic assistance. The ability to do this I have collected during more than 40 years of experience while working with energetic fields of peoples. All you have to do is use all of that and try to find that one faithful spot. Instead of using a pendulum, I suggest you use your own palm, i.e. lightly sway your hand along the entire strip, at approximately 5 cm above the surface. There should be no tension. Do it as if you are playing, until you feel that, at some point, you are permeated by a light gust. What type of gust? This energetic impact may be individual to all of us, but eventually it always leads us to the location of that faithful point. Mark the said spot by putting a pebble or any other object on it and try to estimate the age you were when this happened. It will not be hard. Then you have to remember the important decisions you made at that certain period of your life. This is the key to solving your problem. Oftentimes, it is the key that opens the heavy doors leading outside of the prison your disease has put you in.

## STATE OF PERFECT EXISTENCE

All of these things are extremely important, but it is only the beginning of your escape. Even though the start is quite clear, it still leaves a person with a feeling of vagueness and uncertainty. There is an impression that you have encountered a "bloodless" or even "powerless" theory. Something essential is missing. What is this thing? Indeed, the thing that is missing is a STATE, necessary for this subtle system to come to life, start its palpable vibrations and becoming active. What is this state? I call the method of entering this state the "wide viewing" method. It is very easy to do – before starting your experimentation with testing, calm down, sit down in a comfortable position and start looking through a window. Start watching the clouds, the birds, the trees and the entire vibrating **world of the Creator.** At the same time, use your peripheral vision to observe the room you are in. Widen your gaze in such a way that would enable you to easily see the walls, the ceiling, the floor of your room and the view outside **all at once.** Put effort into maintaining this state of wide and deep observation. It will be enjoyable, as suddenly you will feel peace, relaxation and stability overflowing you. Pay attention – one can live in this peaceful state FOR THE REST OF THEIR LIVES, as this is actually a STATE OF PERFECT EXISTENCE. This is the state that Jesus always wished upon all the people with his words "Peace be with you". Having experienced this surge of peace, you are now ready to take the test. You are up for a surprise, as the signal will now be stronger, you will be in an elevated mood and your inner being will be filled with pleasant delicate excitement.

Let's try to answer the following question: what has triggered this change? As the change had to be extremely deep. A person's visual instrument, their eyes, have taken on a task of dramatically increased observation. It is not difficult to understand that when the flow of information to the brain is increased in such a way, there could come a limit, when the analytical mechanism of the brain is able to act only on the verge of its capabilities. After this limit is crossed, the brain stops analyzing and delves deep into a serene state of general **perception** and becomes only an observer. This state of the brain is the aim professed in all spiritual teachings around the world. People try to achieve it through meditation, mantras, rhythmical repetition of phrases from prayers and many other techniques. The technique I propose is the simplest and most important one, as after making your brain stop in such a way, it retains your possibility to communicate with surrounding on usual way. This state can become continuous. It can simply be a way to live one's life. In this specific case of testing, it is a great tool to stabilize the process of the test. Instead of hectically trying to use your constantly errant and restless brain, the state assists in analyzing situations through momentary PERCEPTION in a state of total peace. In order to reveal the entire spectrum of this method and its operation, at first, we must ask a surprising (for most) question: how many eyes does a human being have? Many will smile and simply answer "two", others, having thought of the popular theory about "the third eye" that has originated in India, will reply "three". But I am going to surprise you: according to my research, a person has six eyes. And yes, I am going to prove this statement. In order to understand what I am talking about, do an experiment. Look around the room you are in. Then think about another room in some other place that you like. It can be at your summer house, at your friends' or parents' homes – it does not matter. Imagine that room far away from you. You use your imagination numerous times throughout the day, without even thinking that you are able to be in two places at the same time and see them both perfectly. One you can see with your physical eyes, and the other – with your, let's call them, SPIRITUAL eyes. The view through your Spiritual eyes is just as spatial and colorful as through your physical eyes, and the latter shows that you are watching it not with one, but two eyes – just like while observing something in a physical sense. This is reality, accept it. If you do, it becomes easy to comprehend that you constantly use four full-fledged eyes. While applying the expanded vision method, you can use physical and spiritual eyes both and add some positive factors to the state you are in. Let's say, when you are imagining yourself in an environment that you like, for instance, in nature, in a favorite spot in the city, at your beloved home, etc. Being in that state, it will only strengthen the feelings of peace and harmony. Well, but what about two more eyes? This is a bit more complicated issue. Let's start from the simplest and universally acceptable concept that your Father-Creator is INSIDE OF YOU. It manifests in each of us as a stream of life, as a force that enables all vital processes, called the Spirit. Here is another question for you: is the Creator-God inside of you blind? Of course not. He has created us according to His image, so, just like us, He has two eyes. And now a very hypothetical question: can a true believer and a loving child ask their beloved Father-Creator for a gift – to let them look at any situation or subject you interested in, through the Creator's eyes? Everybody is allowed to ask. However, it is not clear whether you will receive a positive reply and how it can manifest in you. Everybody is entitled to have an opinion about that. Nonetheless, it is obvious that the possibility of such a question in terms of the relationship between the Creator and His child is very simple and does not violate any sacred laws. So here you go – two more eyes inside of us that are the most important ones. The ones that see us constantly, caress us in their caring gaze, protect, love, guard and teach us: all forms of knowing are in you, as "I'm in you". Ask and you will receive an answer. Knock, and the door will open.

## DEPRESSION

The previously discussed expanded vision method, which helps to achieve direct communication with the Creator-God inside of us, may become an excellent instrument of treating one of the most common mental disorders, i.e. depression. It is obvious that when a person considers their mind the only tool of communication with themselves and analyzes the function of their mind through their efforts to "teach the mind to be smart", sooner or later they will reach a dead end. Unable to perform this function, the mind blocks itself. However, it has become evident that the solution to this problem is much simpler: a patient must be taught to enter the STATE OF PERFECT EXISTENCE. This effort does not require forcing the activity of the mind or activating the latter while "trying to teach one's mind to behave differently". Vice versa, a person has to engage in simple physical activity, the goal of which is to learn how to maintain the expanded vision in a stable way. This exercise does not require anything from the mind itself. Instead, it provides the latter with peacefulness, rest and a constant state of pleasant tranquility. At the same time, a person discovers the internal omniscience phenomenon that comes from the origin of the Spirit and is superb and immeasurably deeper than the mind. It assists in answering internal questions of an individual by applying the method of momentary perception instead of a hectic analysis. Having experienced it at least once, the patient no longer wants to go back to the previous state of their mind "running towards nowhere". This is a path that harmonizes the intrinsic mental and spiritual structures without any attempt to explain or force them. In other words, it is a path towards healing.

Try to enter the SPE (State of Perfect Existence) as frequently as you can. Remember, while being in this state, nothing changes externally – you remain YOU. You will continue to work, perform your household chores, communicate with others – everything will carry on as usual, but in a different, expanded and multidimensional field. You will start seeing gradual positive changes in the quality of your life. You will enter a stable peaceful state and may suddenly feel a need to create something – try it out. Each and every one of us has a soul that the Creator has filled with talents and abilities. Start rummaging through it. It could be the start of a totally different life. Be sure – the things that are happening to you will undoubtedly change your relation to the surroundings. Little by little, by expressing yourself and teaching others to do the same, you will gain respect. You might even start a new profession that could become your source of revenue. It is really worth it – do, not miss out on an opportunity.

And for those who will follow this path by choosing a pendulum as a testing instrument, I highly recommend using a worldwide known Karnak pendulum. Its name comes from a valley in Egypt, where archeological diggings took place. It was in the Karnak valley that a prototype of a bronze pendulum was found in a grave of a pharaoh's high priest. It is believed that such "all knowing" pendulums were used to build the pyramids. The length of the pendulum can be different. The most popular ones are 40 – 60 mm long. Whichever length you choose, the most important thing are the right proportions of the main parts.

The method described is universal, as you can use it to solve any kind of problems in your life. Use your imagination and ingenuity and always apply the same principle.

Now, getting back to the treatment of cancer, the following actions ought to be quite simple. After finding that moment in life when you made a critical mistake, and marking the time of that moment, i.e. the year, the month and maybe even the day (the test enables to determine it very specifically), start the analysis – what was that faithful mistake? Having entered the realm of this contemplation, I stopped for a long period of time. Everybody will do the same – I have no doubts. When you start analyzing your life, the area under investigation seems extremely expansive. However, in this case, the same test field will come to your assistance. Test every past event or thought that comes into your head based on the same "Yes/No" principle. Do it many times, until you get an unambiguous "yes" answer several times. The next step is to perform repentance and make a confession directly to the Creator-God. You have to do this only once. Your Father is full of mercy. Sincere repentance is always the right answer. Trust Him. After doing all of these recommended things, positive changes typically manifest immediately after you are forgiven. Fear disappears, you are overcome with peace, and, during the next several days, you start noticing changes in the course of your disease. Tumors start shrinking, pain vanishes together with metastases. However, all these changes must be overseen applying conventional medical measures.

## THE MIND

The mind is absolute. It does not have a location. It is a substance that exists everywhere – just like space does. At the same time, it is an action program, controlled entirely only by the force that has created it, i.e. the Creator-God. The brains of all live beings can be compared to a hard drive in a computer. It is an intermediary which absorbs as many of the mind program elements as its software capabilities allow. At the same time, the brain is an autonomously evolving structure that, while developing its analytical skills, expands and tries to dominate everything around it.

A developed mind is characterized by expansion. Due to its expansive nature, the mind seeks to control all accessible physical, mental and emotional fields of the personality. The field of feelings is treated in an especially aggressive way, as the mind tries to control and subdue them. Oftentimes, an individual mind seeks to realize its aggressive nature outside the limits of its physical personality, by trying to exert control on other individuals and their physical, mental and emotional powers. During this process, an individual mind comes across only one substance that is able to limit its expansion in a natural way, i.e. the Creator-God inside of us, manifested and recognized by us as the Spirit. The mind is unable to analyze or control the Spirit, because the former has been created and limited by the latter. In many cases, the result of an individual mind trying to analyze, get to know and exert control over the substance of the Spirit is mental impairment and disintegration of the components that constitute the mind. The relation of the mind and the Spirit in each individual is subtly regulated by the origin of the Spirit. If an individual develops in the right way, they start intuitively comprehending the essence of these origins and deliberately try to limit the expressions of the aggressive expansive nature of the mind. While retreating from the inferences dictated by the mind and the jungle of regulated cognition, an individual starts trusting the intuitive relation with the Spirit, i.e. the Creator's substance inside of us, more and more. These efforts are always accompanied by various subtle gifts, the most important of which is higher-level cognition, i.e. momentary perception instead of hectic analysis, or the omniscience phenomenon. Being on this path, the ones who excessively trust the power of the mind, come across undoubtedly purposive and misleading limitations of the mind. Having acquired an aggressively materialistic worldview, science has shot itself in the foot. With the help of intellectual analysis, it has created numerous miracles of technology, but up until now has not been able to notice and acknowledge the source of all life – the existence of the Spirit or the Creator-God inside of us. In the same manner, many phenomena discussed in this book, especially the existence and the function of the Creator-God or the Spirit center inside of us, remain a total secret for science and communities that live affected by its arguments. For now, the phenomenon of feelings has also been neglected by scientific research. In order for these phenomena to be researched and their origins and activity investigated, the "scientific" negation of the existence and the activity of the Spirit or the Creator-God inside of us must be abandoned. Each person can learn the subtle emotional language of destiny and, having acknowledged the priority of the Spirit, trust the latter while moving towards their own destiny. The limitations of our perceptive abilities in no way allows us to formulate absurd theories that God does not exist, that living beings are created and developed by some sort of "environment" and "random conditions". Chaos can only create chaos. Any harmonious and cyclically repetitive phenomena, e.g. life, can come only from a higher-level analogue that creates willed impulses for this process to happen. Science has always been and will always be just a constantly changing instrument of human cognition. The "scientific" statement that God does not exist is no different from the famous phrase once said by a fictional character of Ostap Bender in the novel *The Twelve Chairs*: "There is no God – that's a medical fact!"

Getting back to the aforementioned omniscience phenomenon and its mode of operation, it is essential to understand that it does not result from a developed power of the mind. It is a form of knowing that lies in the phenomenon of the Spirit or the Creator-God inside of us, who, if asked a question – provided our mind does not interfere – will send knowledge into the field of consciousness. After a certain period of time, it comes as a clear reply to a previously asked question. All questions and answers are automatically filtered through a moral filter of the Spirit or the Creator inside of us, and an individual is only allowed to get to know things that do not violate other persons and correspond to what the one who is giving the question has earned in their path of destiny. As one can see, in this case, once again, the all-embracing hand of the Creator-God performs the role of the subtlest judge. In the structure of destiny, it acts unerringly. A message, purified through the Creator's filter, received in the form of direct intuitive cognition, is of the greatest value. Usually, an individual will accept it with immense joy. After that, the road back to the field where the mind dominates and controls everything, is closed forever. However, this does not shut the function of the mind down. The mind becomes an instrument, subordinate to a higher-level form of cognition. When the interaction of these two structures develops further, a phenomenon called enlightenment can occur in the field of the human Soul. The latter means total domination of the Spirit substance in the field of the soul, and a signal that the growth of the soul has surpassed the equator of cognition. The goal of the Soul's existence here on earth has been reached. At that moment, the Spirit substance permeates the entire being of a person and fill it with a perfect feeling of fruition. The physical life of an individual goes on, but the individual changes. The motivation of all of their actions acquires a glow – it is an ability to recognize the ideal truth. While continuing their path of life, a person acquires a glow as well, often felt or even seen by others. Their actions and impact on the surroundings increase dramatically, but they stay the same, maintain the majority of their personal traits and carry on with their usual functions in the society and family. However, it is, indeed, the destiny of the chosen ones. Can the enlightenment phenomenon be considered a goal? If so, how can it be achieved? The answer is simple: yes, enlightenment is the natural goal of all people. Obscure to many, it is intuitively understood and pursued by others. There is only one way – to quit all forms of intoxication, make one's creative pursuits a priority and realize their abilities and talents, looking for direct inspiration in the realm of the Spirit. There are no untalented people. The Spirit is open and generous to everybody, but the path becomes clear only to those who take it. And it is totally not important, whether we are talking about a huge radiant talent who is able to make nations fall under their feet or a barely noticeable euphoria of a village gardener. Nonetheless, even if one follows this plan, there is no guarantee that you will ever reach enlightenment. This depends on your master, the Creator, and His actions are often unpredictable. However, there is a reliable and simple path that gradually leads towards enlightenment. It is partial enlightenment that takes place in the creative realm of an individuality's expression, when the highest creative inspiration is reached. A partly enlightened personality perceives an event as euphoria, a perfect feeling of nirvana that takes place when one's pursuits are achieved. At the same time, a person always understands that this is not complete enlightenment. If these partial phenomena keep repeating, total enlightenment can occur, and a person will always be able to recognize it.

A fairly common event is the induction of the enlightenment phenomenon. This usually happens when a person, who has already experienced total enlightenment, expresses themselves in public and in some way infects the ones who are listening with their influence. This type of feeling is typically publicly created by souls who have been gifted with a special talent, i.e. scientists giving public speeches, actors, musicians, preachers and prophets. This publication will also disperse an aura of enlightenment, as its author has experienced one. It may seem that, by providing this reasoning, I devalue the mind and minimize the role it has played in the development of personality and society. The function of the mind is absolutely positive and necessary for the activity of life forms of all levels. However, it cannot be assessed by separating it from the accompanying spiritual-emotional phenomenon that controls mental activity. It always manifests itself as a leading and delicately dictating force of feeling. In the path of life, both of these sources – mind and feeling – must interact in harmony. The Creator does not perceive neither of them as being more important. Nevertheless, if the mind starts dominating, drastic negative disproportions are inevitable. All most aggressive and most devastating social order theories were created based on logical reasoning. Modern fascism and communism, religious discord theories nowadays and in the Middle Ages were always able to find – and still do – arguments that drive the masses to plunge themselves into madness.

What function does the mind of individuals who have experienced enlightenment have? The activity of the mind remains full-fledged, but it starts, in a sense, pulsating. The mind dominates when it is necessary in terms of a certain situation (e.g., when an individual is studying), but moves to the periphery when it is not needed. In this case, a person delves into a pleasant state of absolute perception. This perception encompasses all spheres of the person's interests and is reminiscent of the feeling of peace one gets while meditating. This is how the State of Perfect Existence (described herein) manifests. However, while in this state, the person is in total control of their practical activities as well.

It is in a way an intrinsic vision, which helps to distinguish priorities and assist in finding the most rational solutions with ease. This internal state represents a perfect field of personal creation.

## POLLUTION OF SUBCONSCIOUSNESS

All information you let into your consciousness accumulates and piles up. Consciousness can only retain a limited amount of information. When these limits are reached, from the field of consciousness, information travels to an immensely larger reservoir, i.e. subconsciousness. The same can be seen in computers, but the processes in the informational circulation of human consciousness and subconsciousness differ in one very important way: information, transferred into subconsciousness, is packaged in FEELINGS. Thus, the information that travels from consciousness to subconsciousness as emotional components dissolves in the general space of the subconsciousness and, due to this, affects the general quality of its content. Depending on the positivity or negativity of the feeling that is being transferred, these flows can either illuminate the subconsciousness in a positive way, or pollute it. This happens when this space, purposefully or not, is filled with negative feelings being transferred, i.e. anger, aggression, fear and so on. In the general subconscious space, feelings coalesce and accumulate. Thus, if they are negative, it creates a significant problem for the master of this field – the Creator. The general subconscious space is His Garden, the world of His existence and control, which, unfortunately, cannot be polluted without any consequences. If a person, who is polluting this space with negative feelings, exceeds the level of pollution allowed, they will be punished. Depending on the characteristics and intensity of the pollution, the punishments can be indeed drastic. For example, they can take the form of depression, injuries during accidents, attacks of criminals, mental diseases and, finally, cancer. All of us have that potential of the allowed and safe pollution level. We cannot, however, asses it in a physical sense, weigh, measure its volume, see its color and so on, but we can evaluate the percentage of the negativity we have already created in subconsciousness. Let's assume that the critical pollution level that invokes punishment is somewhere between 80%100%. Well, let's look at the test field. There is 0 on the left, 100% on the right, and a wonderful opportunity right now for you to detect the level of pollution that has accumulated in your subconscious field. Do this by lightly swinging your hand above the test strip. Feal importance of the moment! It is somewhere between 0 and 100%. Is it interesting? Of course, but scary nonetheless. The testing principle is exceedingly simple and clear. It cannot be a lie. If the level of your subconsciousness pollution does not exceed 50%, there is no need to worry. It does not pose any direct danger, but encourages to think about what you are doing wrong, if half of the fatal amount is already there. Let me give you an example: imagine a young woman, who was born and has been living with physical defects. Due to this, she feels a lot of desperation and starts blaming her parents, her destiny, feels unhappy and thinks that this is totally unfair. It turns out that this is enough for all this dissatisfaction to transform into intense negativity, constantly flowing to her subconsciousness. In this case, the critical level of negativity starts forming at a very young age and thus creates a threat of serious punishments. If the same girl stopped concentrating on defects and would start pursuing self-realization, let's say, by becoming a poet, a writer, a singer or a physician – the problem would disappear. The girl would break through the complex of negative feelings and would start sending positive feelings to her subconsciousness, counterbalancing the already accumulated negativity. This is how it works. Different people may experience it differently, but the main principle is the same for all. Thus, everybody should take on the task of detecting the percentage of their subconscious pollution. Having achieved that, you can do it for other people, e.g. your children, parents, friends, acquaintances and public personalities as well. It is a normal "Practice of Karma". You are no longer a total rookie in this field. Moreover, generally speaking, under the right circumstances, you can use this knowledge to avoid an upcoming personal catastrophe. I wish that upon everybody.

## APTITUDES AND TALENTS

The most valuable and most dangerous gift from God and a tool of destiny is our aptitudes, especially their highest form, i.e. talents. It is clear why they are valuable, but why are they dangerous? We will understand this through a deeper analysis of what has already been mentioned earlier, the structure of a soul. The soul of any human being is the result of the Creator-God's activity. By incorporating the functions of the spiritual Father and Mother, the Creator looks at His children the way we see ours. This is undoubtedly dominated by love and a wish for the child to grow, i.e. for them to become physically strong, collect knowledge, develop emotional intellect, intelligence and spirituality. In order for the soul to grow, the Creator gives us instruments, the most important of which are our aptitudes or talents. It is essential to understand that a person cannot create any aptitudes, let alone talent, inside themselves or others. A soul can only develop what has already been given to it or others. Moreover, it is necessary to realize one obvious truth: we are God's creative projects, and we can only become our true selves if we accomplish

God's creative plan, in simpler terms, the task of growth that has been planned for us. What does it mean to become our true selves? Unlike our earthly parents, the Creator-God can provide His children with a priceless gift – immortality, i.e. to make our Soul or our individuality eternal. This statement can be found in almost all religious and spiritual teachings, but usually they do not mention the fact that the soul is responsible for what we try to appropriate, i.e. our aptitudes and talents – tools of destiny, created by God and given to us. This type of behavior is fundamentally wrong. Such priceless gifts as aptitudes (and especially talents) are given to us not as a present that we can treat as we like, but rather as a loan for our life journey. This journey can be successful only if we treat God's gifts responsibly.

> The strangest and biggest human secret is the human being itself, i.e. their inner world. There is a very small number of people who can see their aptitudes clearly and are able to develop and use them efficiently. At the same time, people who do not have aptitudes do not exist. There is nothing new in my statement that the Creator-God (just as we do with our children) follows His children's actions with a loving but at the same time controlling gaze. He sees how we treat His most delicate and most valuable gift that determines the quality of our soul – our aptitudes. Imagine, what would you do, if, having received an expensive and beautiful toy, your child started breaking it? Of course, it is highly likely that many parents would take it away and maybe give it to some other child. Thus, if we ignore, misuse or mistreat them, the Creator is also sometimes forced to take our toys – our aptitudes – away from us. The

worst thing is that usually He is able to do it only by taking our life together with them. That is why the toys gifted by God is not only valuable but dangerous as well.

There is an infinite number of CEOs working as janitors, composers selling old junk, poets who steal for a living, mathematicians who spend their days in casinos and so on. All of their inner worlds are plagued with relentlessly growing anxiety and dissatisfaction with themselves. This feeling is unbearable; thus, the soul tries to get free from it and deaden it with pleasure and intoxication. However, it is impossible. The feeling of dissatisfaction is constantly flowing into the subconsciousness. The process of subconscious pollution starts, and lasts only till the critical concentration level is achieved. After that, the tools of destiny start playing their role, the most common of which being depression. It is not difficult to understand why treatment in the form of activating consciousness with artificial methods does not work. Having fallen into this trap, a person usually tries easily accessible things that generate good feeling, i.e. alcohol, cigarettes, drugs, excessive sex with multiple partners and so on. Over time, the amount needed to feel better constantly grows. This road leads to nowhere. This only leads to irreversibly losing the most precious thing given to us – the possibility to grow by using Creator-given abilities. Usually people who keep losing themselves in the described way have many typical mental and physiological disorders. One of the most severe forms of destiny punishments is cancer. For an attentive reader, the phenomena discussed herein will raise a logical question. Can cancer, received as a punishment and already gaining momentum, be stopped? Or even cured, if the person remembers their natural abilities and starts working on them intensely? The answer is – yes, without a doubt. This is one of the most important paths towards a patient's possible positive spiritual and physical transformation, in simpler terms – an instrument of treatment. If a person starts walking this path, cancer oftentimes disappears.

## CANCER

Almost forty years ago, in my attempt to help my son who had immense health problems (progressive muscular atrophy), I came face to face with the total helplessness of the conventional medicine. Having understood that the traditional medical methods are useless, I started looking for nonconventional treatment. I mastered the bioenergy correction method which was already quite well-known at that time. Later, I found that it was the only way to help my son feel better. Unfortunately, it could not cure him. The life of my son, who already was not able to move without a wheelchair, was brightened by a friendship with a good-hearted girl, named Alma. The events that followed were extremely difficult for my son to accept. The said girl got cancer and died shortly after. I tried to help her but, unfortunately, my efforts did not have any results. The ruthless phenomenon of this disease and its horrible power manifested in its entirety right in front of our eyes. It was a horrible time for my son. This encouraged me to make a decision to try to reveal the secret of this disease, find the right key and defeat it. This process has not ended yet. However, now I can say that I have completed my task. The fateful shift, enabled by my unique past practices, happened several years ago.

For many years, while travelling around the globe, I used professional aura photography equipment. I took thousands of pictures and mastered the intuitive interpretation of the colors and forms of aura. Finally, I learned how to see this subtle glow with my naked eye and even affect the aura of the person I was watching. Then I started teaching other people the techniques of directly watching auras. This unique practice led me towards an exceptional moment, when I understood that, during my contact with patients, multichannel communication in the field of aura takes place. And it is undoubtedly related to various diseases people have. This revelation helped me to see a light at the end of the tunnel. These thoughts encouraged me to consciously act in the field of multichannel aura circulation while communicating with patients directly. During each visit, I started sitting my patients down into a chair in front of a brightly-lit smooth wall, painted in a light pastel color. This environment was ideal for watching auras. I started doing it during all conversations and correction sessions – it became a usual practice for me. I did this intuitively, trying to pursue a goal that was still quite obscure to me. My intuition kept telling me that if I keep walking down this path and acquire enough experience, I could reveal unexpected and extremely important phenomena that were happening during the observations.

A very important circumstance of these experimentations was the fact that the observations always took place while communicating with a patient at the same time.

*The message sent by my intuition turned out to be completely true. During these wonderful contacts with patients, fascinating patterns of colors and forms I kept seeing in their auras helped me enter a state of perfect connection with the people in front of me. However, I soon discovered that this vibrating and glowing connection is multidimensional.*

I felt that in parallel with communication with a patient, pulsating colorful connection was being developed with something else as well. Oftentimes, the things my patients used to say or complain about, also their arguments did not correspond to the panoramic play of the aura I was seeing. I felt like another personality was trying to join the conversation. Very soon I was able to come up with a simple and clear explanation of this exciting phenomenon: I was speaking not only to the patient, but to the actively engaged segment that connects us all – the Creator-God inside us!!! However, it took me some time to finally make the last step towards this fascinating concept, which meant that the Creator was offering a dialogue! He was expressing himself with visual and quite understandable color patterns and offered His input while trying to solve the problems of the person who came in. In other words, the Creator-God wanted to speak to us directly! Not through verbal language but through radiance. That was not too difficult to interpret. This was his amazing way of communication!!! This "language" was manifesting not only via the ever-changing fascinating colors but subtle feelings as well. And those feelings could always be interpreted as agreement, doubt or disagreement with both parties of the conversation, i.e. the ideas and thoughts of myself and my guest. As my experience grew, I was able to clearly distinguish among the impacts the different parties to the conversation were making on the final result. The amazing thing was that I, a person who was used to treating people by willfully sending energy currents to my patients, while applying the method I had learned during the years and years of healing practice, had to gradually leave the treatment process. I had to give up my place so that an immeasurably more powerful sacred source – the Creator – could act. Amazed, I did this with immense satisfaction. Treatment results did not suffer but, on the contrary, became immensely more powerful. Oftentimes, the only way I could describe that was a miracle. Observing and participating in this process was similar to inner birth. In a totally new field of perception and feeling, I slowly but clearly understood that I was learning a new and unique language. A direct language with the Creator. Apart from experiencing an exciting miracle, during this process, I was able to directly witness and get to know how the subtlest and strongest of all existing powers, the Creator-God, works. The only thing left to do was to name the communication method I had discovered. I decided to call this instrument of communicating with the Creator language OMEGA. I accepted that I had made all these discoveries only because I was led by Him. This interaction provided me with enormous and unique help while solving practical matters in specific cases of treatment. The entire process and His language that was radiating unworldly colors meant only one thing: being on this path, one has to be absolutely sincere, as this experience must be cherished as the most sacred of all. It could only be experienced and used if your heart was benevolent, pure and open. The miraculous moments of communicating with the Creator-God and the discovery of His amazing language provided me with an exciting and obvious understanding that this was the key I was looking for so intensely, the key that would open the doors to the most secret of all earthly mysteries, the treatment of cancer being one of them! I understood that there was one more step to take. I had to cure a specific patient, so that the entirety of all circumstances could confirm or refute the propriety of this path. This could only happen while treating a patient, who had undergone all medical testing that had confirmed their cancer diagnosis, but had not started the treatment process yet. I did not have to wait for long.

## A SIGN

A young woman contacted me. She was about forty years old. Several tumors had been found in her breasts. After a biopsy, physicians diagnosed cancer. The woman's eyes were filled with fear. I asked her, "Have you received any treatment?"

"Not yet. An operation has been scheduled."

"Do you believe in God?"

"Oh, yes. I go to church regularly. Maybe, I could practice my faith more often, but I do feel inner peace. Yes, I'm a devoted believer."

"I've just tested you. The Creator says that, unfortunately, you are not a believer."

"I don't understand."

"Do you agree that God is inside of you, that it is Him who generates your vital energy, watches over you constantly and protects you from fatal diseases?"

"Ok, I understand your question now. You know, it is hard to believe that he's meticulously watching me. And, if he protects me from fatal diseases, how come I have cancer?"

"Do you have children?"

"Yes."

"Imagine a situation: you are in a room together with your children, but they barely notice you, you receive zero attention from them. Would you like that?"

"Of course, not."

"What if it's constant, let's say, it lasts for a lifetime? Wouldn't you feel disappointed and look the other way?"

"It hurts to even think about that. I don't know what I would do."

"It hurts God, too. Especially, when He feels ignored by one of His children. You do agree that you, just like any other person, are a child of God? The fact that you ignore the existence of your spiritual Father-God inside of you is enough to be abandoned. It is enough to lose His protection."

"And this is the reason why I have cancer?"

"Maybe, not the single, but an extremely important one. God tells us: I don't need anything special from you except one thing – love me the way I love you. So, tell me this: do you love God more than yourself, more than your children?"

"Well, you know… More than my children?"

"Exactly. It provides a necessary connection with God, because it is the only way for you and your children to be protected against disasters. Protected or not."

"What should I do?"

"Right now, right here, you must pray and apologize to God, and try to open yourself to Him, who is right there inside of you, below your heart. People usually call it Spirit. Do you agree to do that? Right now."

"Yes."

"Would you mind, if I prayed together with you and strengthened your plea?"

"No, of course, not."

> Silence ensues. I watch the woman's aura. At one point, there's a flash and the aura expand. The woman closes her eyes, sways lightly and smiles. I do not bother her. I already know that God has forgiven her. An amazing feeling washes over me.

This is only a part of the conversation that happened. However, it is the most important part. Later on, we analyzed other, smaller transgressions that happened in her life. The woman had to ask for God's forgiveness several more times. And she received it each time. The list of her mistakes became shorter and shorter. She felt at peace.

> During the entire process, I tried my best not to interfere with her treatment with any techniques known to me. I left the entire process to a force immeasurably more powerful than me – the Creator.

I knew that she was cured during this session. She was already free of cancer. I told her this. Shaking her head, she did not believe me. I told her the same thing I always tell patients in a situation like this, "Don't take my word for it. Go to your physicians and demand for additional testing. It is necessary for them to confirm what I've just told you."

"It's not necessary. My operation has been scheduled. They are going to test the tissue taken out in a laboratory. As far as I understand, I have to believe that these tests will show that I am cancer free?"

"This no longer depends on your opinion or your fears. There is no cancer inside of you anymore. The medical tests are going to inevitably show that."

The woman left. I saw her off with a smile – she was fighting off tears but glowing at the same time. I saw that it was really difficult for her to take the new reality in.

> Everything what I had said was proven to be true. The laboratory testing of the dissected tissue provided a different outcome compared to the histological samples that had been taken out during a previous biopsy. There were no cancerous cells detected.

Shortly after, she visited me once again. The woman looked great. She told me that the doctors were not at all happy with the wonderful results of the tests performed on the tissue dissected after the operation. They interpreted it as a random mistake and suggested continuing the treatment based on the previous testing. They demanded that the chemotherapy prescribed earlier would take place. The woman disagreed. It took a lot of relentless convincing for her to agree to undergo a minimal radiology procedure on her breasts. Even though there was no need for that, the procedure was performed. She was completely healthy. By the way, she is a doctor herself.

## CREATOR – HUMAN. DIRECT COMMUNICATION

This specific case proved without a shadow of a doubt the efficiency of this new method that entails direct communication with the Creator-God inside of us. At first, the purpose of the book *"The Practice of Karma. The End to the Era of Cancer?"* was to present the discovery of this new way of treating of cancer. However, as the time passed by, it became increasingly evident to me that the quest to uncover the secrets of cancer has brought me really close to a much bigger discovery.

> The methods discovered have revealed paths towards direct communication between the CREATOR and a HUMAN BEING, the value of which has no limits!!! This can become a key to solving the most challenging problems of human existence and everyday life.

As you can see, the self-help method described in the book is very simple – a search for mistakes and, eventually, treatment. The only thing required from the patient is sincere repentance and prayer. This method can always be applied in parallel with conventional medical treatment. The physicians supervising the patient will always have to say the final word, whether the patient has been cured or not. In order to introduce these new concepts and provide this field with a possibility to check the statements made, I will do my best to make this publication known in the medical community. I am always open to cooperation and I would gladly participate in any medical research.

Step by step moving closer to my discoveries, I have always counted on technical–engineering intuition alone. I do not believe in anything that cannot be verified. Meanwhile, my intuition tells me that the field of multichannel glowing communication can be seen not only through sensitive eyes used to observing such phenomena, but that its visualization could be created using technical means as well. The said processes could be recorded by using modern equipment. This would enable a deeper analysis of the processes, collection of data and scientific assessment. I would gladly share my thoughts, experience and knowledge, if approached by a person or an organization that has adequate resources and a desire to engage in such investigation. All my doors are open.

In addition, the methods to look for ways how to help yourself or others, discussed in *"The Practice of Karma"*, will inevitably lead each reader towards strengthening their inner intuitive powers. In any case, this path will provide priceless experience while moving towards the omniscience phenomenon. It lies inside every human being, in the realm of the Spirit, and, having acquired enough experience, can transform into clairvoyance. In terms of spiritual practices, there are no deeper, more fascinating or more enchanting methods than the revelation of your intrinsic clairvoyance abilities. By applying the unique program described in the present book, you can enter and analyze all paths of cognition. The field of cognition has no limits – just like life itself. May your journey be fulfilling.


## THE SPECTRAL RESONANCE OF THE CRONE

This concept is new. There have been many circumstances that encouraged me to introduce it. The first of them was knowing that it is "a blind spot" in the field of human structure cognition. An additional argument has been the Covid-19 pandemic currently shattering the globe. In order to understand and treat many deadly diseases, the content of the said concept must be revealed. This is interconnected with both – conventional medical means and spiritual treatment methods alike, and significant in the context of Covid-19 virus attacks, Lyme disease and all types of encephalitis.

What am I talking about? I am talking about the most sensitive organ in human body, i.e. the brain. I do not have enough anatomical or medical knowledge to comment on or assess the existing scientific research of the structure of the brain. I am conducting my own research using the methods described herein, which do not entail medical evaluation aspects of the brain activity. The laws and activity patterns that I have detected operate in the realm of a person as a spiritual being, created by the Higher Analogue or the Creator. In the said realm, the importance of brain activity could hardly be overestimated. The brain is the center of existence and various conscious and vegetative processes in the body. Only when this center operates perfectly, can existence be harmonious and comprehensive.

> The aforementioned concept of spectral crown resonance has been created in order to explain the existing phenomenon of a resonant relation between the minds of the Creator and a Human Being. The Creator's dictating structure and the structures of the person's brain and mind are radiating vibration complexes of unimaginable intricacy. The controlling and dictating vibration complex of the Creator's Mind is perfect. By virtue of resonance, it permeates the minds and their physical analogues – the brains – of all people.

One does not have to unconditionally obey to the dictating mind of the Creator. A person's free will always has a priority. Even a person who is perfectly aware of the resonant vibrations of the Creator's mind can choose to conform to them or ignore them whatsoever. The person can choose other vibration models, if they seem more appealing. The existential space is full of them. There are various possible combinations, in which a human mind can conform to several sources of vibrations that could be fighting with each other or interacting. In case of a perfect interaction, a full-fledged resonant connection between the Creator and the person is achieved. It manifests in the entire chromatic spectrum of vibrations and creates a perfect interaction, when the human mind conforms and responds to the vibrations of the Creator's mind.

> In which case, the space that includes the brain, the gap between the brain and the scull and the tissues of the scull itself are gradually filled with wonderful structure of glowing plasma, sent by the Creator. I named it the "crown". It is a layer that protects the human brain from the attacks of deadly viruses. And not only that. This layer has many amazing properties. First of all, a person who has a full-fledged "crown" can use it as a treatment instrument. This substance has no limits, it obeys the commands of thinking and feeling, and, after travelling limitless distances, can immediately reach a person asking for help anywhere on the planet. The author of this book learned about this phenomenon and acquired a power to purposefully use its potential after the enlightenment he has experienced. I accepted it as a priceless gift from the Creator.

A complete and concentrated "crown" radiates and can be seen in the color spectrum. People with sensitive eyes are often able to notice it. The term "spectral" is a reference to color. Each person's brain forms its own crown and, depending on spiritual connections and activity priorities, the crown can acquire various colors that represent all human energy centers.

> Having an absolute protective power, the strongest of the all is the Creator's crown, which is white. As we all know, white is the sum of all colors.

All other colors of the crown can have stronger or weaker protective and operative effects, but they are always only partial. There are factors that can have a destructive effect on the crown. The most significant of them all are intoxicating substances, i.e. alcohol, drugs and nicotine. Let's conduct a simple test in order to see how alcohol affects the crown. Upon using a certain amount of alcohol, a person feels euphoric. The euphoria lasts only until there is alcohol remaining in the blood stream. Afterwards, the person experiences a hangover. During that time, the person's brain is impacted by poison, i.e. components of alcohol that reach the brain through blood. The said poison remains in the brain for a long time and has a catastrophic effect on the crown. Due to it, subtle plasma energy constructs simply disintegrate. If such a person is attacked by Covid-19, its exposed and unprotected brain is an easy target for the virus. After entering the brain, viruses partially paralyze the respiratory centers, and the infection progresses further on to the lungs, which is oftentimes followed by death. These circumstances easily explain why the amount of Covid-19 deaths is highest in the countries where wine and drugs are widely used.

Meanwhile, a person, who is on a path of spiritual development, eats healthy food and ignores intoxicating substances, strengthens their body's general resistance to all diseases and especially the brain's resistance to viral infections.

Every person can pursue a positive interaction with our Father-Creator. However, each of us walk on our individual paths. In any case, all doors of the Creator are always open to everybody.

## ESCAPE THE COVID-19. Description-3.
*Author of method Arvydas Daskus*

A  l o o k  f r o m  t h e  i n s i d e :

The described methodology has already been tested in Lithuania by author of this method. There was now time and opportunity to join efforts to combating COVID-19 in other countries. I propose to distribute among the medical staff in the hospitals, as well as among the people who have already been infected, the "Spiritual-holistic treatment methodology" section contained within this letter. The proposed methodology is also perfect for disease prevention for those who want to avoid getting infected or recover easily if you become infected.

Forty years of experience using the Creator's gift, a phenomenon of clairvoyance, allowed me to carefully analyze the functioning of the virus when the COVID-19 virus began to invade the world. I did this by observing its work not only externally, but also from the inside, using an instrument of clairvoyance. Such observation reveals a completely different picture of how the virus functions than that which is broadcast by the health services. The main activity of the virus is carried out at the very beginning of the infection, during the so-called "dry" period. It begins from losing feelings of taste and smell. At this stage, the virus intensively multiply itself in area of mouth and nose. At the same time, it invades the internal space of skull and attacks the human brain. As a result of this attack, the activity of respiratory centers gets partially paralyzed. And only after this, in an already damaged, poorly functioning breathing system, a direct attack on the lungs follows. After that everything happens as the medical profession sees it. Virus' activity is partially similar (in my view) to the Lyme disease. It is clear that even after revealing this schematic of virus' actions, there are no means to clean up the patient's brains, where the virus has already taken "ownership". Medicine, as far as I know, does not have the measures to put brakes on this process. But my practice shows that, by applying the usual methods of energy correction from the practice of spiritual treatment and using a range of well-known methods from household medicine, excellent results can be achieved in the treatment of the COVID-19 virus. The proposed treatment methodology in no way contradicts the treatment methods currently applied by medical profession. The author of this text does not suggest clashing one method against the other but recommends applying both methods simultaneously. It is a path to success.

Spiritual-holistic treatment methodology.

I suggest applying this method in the earliest phase of the virus' attack. There is no harm in starting to apply it before the testing for infection takes place, right after you start feeling the first symptoms. If you become infected with something else, i.e. not the coronavirus, the methodology will help you to overcome even the ordinary flu and possibly even other forms of encephalitis, such as the Lyme disease. If you have already been tested and diagnosed with COVID-19, the virus has gained momentum and you have breathing problems, it is still not too late for you to join the treatment process proposed in this recommendations package. Positive changes and complete recovery are expected, and they do not depend on the age of the patient, their state or any pre-existing medical conditions. The method can also be valuable for those who are in self-isolation after a contact with an infected person. In any case, it is an active personal action, a treatment, and not just a delay while waiting for a verdict.

P r o p o s e d :

From the very beginning of the treatment, special hygiene of mucous membrane of the nasopharynx is necessary. This is the area most abundant with viruses, where the conditions are favorable for them to breed and travel on – to the bronchi, lungs. The basis of the recommended hygiene procedures is washing the mucous membrane with disinfectant fluid or mouthwash, usually used for rinsing teeth and throat.

Procedure: dilute the mouthwash liquid approximately to concentration 20 – 30 % and, using a long pipette (or a rubber bladder of the children's enema), instill the liquid directly onto the mucous membrane of the nasopharynx through the nose. Do this next to the sink. After cleaning one side, repeat the same with the other side of the nose. The mucous membrane is sensitive to the procedure, but very quickly the unpleasant sensations pass immediately easing the breathing. The procedure is repeated as required.

The effectiveness of mouthwash as the tool against Coronavirus was proven by scientists and presented by PETER DOCKRILL 21/October/2020 in Journal of Medical Virology. Article:

---

"Mouthwash May Help to Neutralize Coronavirus, Experiment with Human Cells Suggests."

As recommend author of this methodology, in order to increase resistance of brain to invasion of virus, Arvydas Daskus propose to listen a special meditation music AD.Mysty3 several times per day. This is a musical track created by the author of this method. The author, Arvydas Daskus, has no musical education or playing skills, but, unexpectedly, while in a deep trance sitting behind the musical instrument, recorded this musical track. Later, slightly altered, the track remained the foundation that conveys to each listener a message of Spirit's healing. One needs to listen to this music through headphones. It can be done while dosing or sleeping. The volume of the music must be medium to low and these musical sounds can also be used to heal children. In this instance, the headphones are placed under the pillow while the child is asleep.

A short extract of this meditational track can be found here:

https://www.youtube.com/watch?v=yyNletKZw5Y&t=11s

2. Every day the author of this program/method, Arvydas Daskus, will treat all users of the methodology directly. Methods of treatment has secret dimension and can't be described. These prayer-healing sessions will take place on distance at a conveniently chosen time.

The application of this entire package of measures usually produces excellent results. There is no research that could answer the question of how effective this program is, but a personal practice suggests that patients usually recover within 1-7 days. With extensive application of this method in parallel with the medical treatment, it is possible to completely eradicate COVID-19. In an instance of re-occurrence, this treatment can always be repeated. Its efficiency will not decrease.

> There is only one exception in the application of this additional treatment: the package will not work if you are using alcohol (no matter what sort and how often), drugs or smoking. In order to use the methodology proposed in this description, first of all, one must stop using poison, stop polluting own body, stop poisoning loved ones and those around them. One must accept the pledge to become an abstinent, never use the mentioned poisons and fulfill this promise until the end of life. Only then one can join this proposed treatment program.

This whole treatment program is free of charge. A small cost will only be applicable and paid by those who are not satisfied with the length of the meditation snippet uploaded on YouTube and who want to purchase a full musical track. The full record can be downloaded here: www.cancerkeylab. org/coronavirus

Cancer Key Lab is open to donations. If the proposed methodology/program has helped you and you would like to thank CKL and the author for the research and work, you can do so by clicking the "Donate" button one the main page (cancerkeylab.org). By donating you not only support the COVID-19 treatment program, but also the continuous development of the cancer prevention and treatment program.

Yours sincerely,

Arvydas Daskus

Author and founder Methodology Cancer Key Lab.

E: info@cancerkeylab.org   Ph: +37068897018

Anyone who needs help can contact the author:

Arvydas Daškus. Tel. +37068897018

El. p.  arvydasdaskus@yahoo.com

Children are prioritized.

The author consults regarding Covid-19, Lyme's disease, all types of encephalitis and other problems. It is not necessary to visit the bioenergotherapist in person, as there is a possibility of remote treatment. Arvydas Daškus commonly uses the remote treatment method, discussed in the chapter Spectral Crown Resonance herein.

The help is provided free of charge.

The author gladly participates in meetings, lectures and training. Please contact the author directly.

The author accepts donations. If you are willing to make a donation that could be used to publish new books or organize meetings, you can do so via a bank transfer to the author's account.

Swedbank, Egidijus Arvydas Daskus, account number: LT137300010112167809

Thank you in advance.

Opinion Regarding COVID-19

Arvydas Daškus, a member of the „Lithuanian

Chamber of Healthy Living and Natural Medicine", a bioenergetotherapist, a healer and writer, presents his opinion regarding the causes of the COVID-19 pandemic and what could be done to stop it.

Nowadays, many people keep asking the same question: what is the real spiritual reason of our planet being under an attack of this unique COVID-19 virus that has already caused a global pandemic? I have been able to answer this question. Now I would like to share my opinion with you. In order to understand this mystery, one has to possess elementary spiritual knowledge about the conscious and the subconscious human mind. It is not difficult to comprehend the limitations of the human consciousness. All the information that travels to the consciousness via the human mind – be it positive or negative – accumulates, and, sooner or later, fills up the space where it is contained. When this happens, the surplus of information is transferred to the general field of the subconscious mind. The information being transferred is never neutral, as it is always "packed" into a certain feeling that can be negative or positive as well. Each person has a critical limit of negative emotional information that can be transferred to the subconscious mind. When the said limit starts getting closer, a person experiences internal stress. Out-of-control anxiety and fear take over, and the environment becomes filled with perceived enemies. This is already a disease. Pay attention: this is how the GENERAL subconsciousness reacts to the surplus contamination reaching a critical threshold. What is this general subconsciousness? It is a hypothetical Force that protects and controls the quality of the planet's consciousness. You can call it however you like – God, Life Generator or the Automated Subconscious Quality Control System. We can think of many more names for it, but the essence of how this General Planetary Controlling Force operates is much more important. It does not allow the contamination of the subconscious beyond a certain limit. Those who cross the said limit are punished severely, usually by contracting grave and deadly diseases.

Now let's discuss the most important thing. The conscious and the subconscious realms and their analogous interaction can be found not only inside each human being but in the essence of our planet as well. In other words, analogous phenomena related to the contamination of the planetary subconscious and punishments for doing the latter are extremely relevant in this case as well. Thus, the COVID-19 situation is a punishment for the contamination levels of the general planetary subconsciousness that have been dramatically exceeded. So, in this context, what are the factors that distort and contaminate the general planetary subconscious so drastically? It is quite symbolic that, in the spiritual realm, the surplus negative information, generated by an individual or the humankind, and flowing into the subconscious is called the SUBCONSCIOUS AGGRESSION. The gradually increasing aggression in individuals, nations and communities needs no proof. It is indisputable. Nonetheless, in this context, it is extremely important to distinguish one extremely dangerous phenomenon, which generates the biggest amount of the subconscious contamination, i.e. the widespread consumption of psychoactive substances. The general field of the planet's consciousness is distorted and unhealthy due to the intoxicants massively consumed by the humankind, i.e. alcohol, nicotine and many types of synthetic and natural drugs. These substances are mostly sought after by young people. Having easily overcome sham prohibitions, they are the most active creators of the distorted, intoxicated and contaminated consciousness. This is a huge disease of the planet. Distorted in the aforementioned way, the general consciousness of humankind accumulates and forwards to the subconscious realm an extremely dangerous, intoxicated and poisonous flow of insanity contamination.

Let's look at the method of COVID-19 operation: entering the body through the respiratory system, the infection affects the throat and the nasopharynx, inhibiting the activity of taste and smell receptors. During the next stage, the virus travels to the brain and starts destroying the basis of life – the autonomic nervous system that controls bodily functions and, primarily, the respiratory functioning. It is often expressed through severe headache and an onset of coughing. The spread of infection ends in a paralysis or deficiency of the respiratory system and, quite often, death. In this case, traditional medicine fails to adequately react to the attack on the brain, where all most significant processes take place. A substantial amount of spiritual practice centers around the knowledge that the brain possesses an inherent plasma coating that protects it against viruses, the so called "crown". However, this coating can be promptly destroyed by psychoactive substances. Each substance (especially alcohol) creates momentary euphoria that is followed by inescapable poisonous hangover. Nowadays, one of the biggest tragedies lies in the fact that conventional medicine ignores this phenomenon and sometimes even tolerates it as "consumption supports economy". I have no doubts that the call for condemning and limiting the said consumption will prompt many users to respond in a similar an alcoholic reacts when someone tries to take the bottle they are clutching to their heart away. This consumption of poison has become an ordinary activity we are all used and to no longer pay any mind to. Consequently, the said insanity has spread, deepened and gradually become prevalent all over the world. For this reason, the reaction in the subconscious realm, i.e. punishment, is totally understandable. This is specifically why the planet has been drowning in a swamp of this unseen virus.

So what is the solution? Vaccination? Medications? Yes, these remedies can affect the virus, but, having all the perspectives of the aforementioned situation in mind, it is hard to believe that a return to the "protected insanity" could be the right solution. On the other hand, it is also possible that the lives already lost could transform into an invaluable lesson learnt. Perhaps, their sacrifice will help to understand that human consciousness is an extremely sensitive and important instrument for any individual as well as the planet itself. While operating inside the realm of our conscious mind, we must take responsibility not only for ourselves, but for our family, loved ones, our community, nation, continent, planet and the Force that has created and controls us, and which, as we all can see now, can punish as much as protect us. The name you give it has no significance whatsoever. Let's start making our way out of this deadly quicksand. The only real solution lies in the intrinsic light and cleanliness of our thoughts and feelings – especially, the two most important of them – Faith and Love. I beckon all people – the younger generation, high-risk elderly people, physicians and government officials – to take this path, as this is the only way out.

This MESSAGE is universal. It is a signpost. In an effort to strive for change, it can be accepted and followed by all – planetary management institutions, governments and parliaments of different countries, managing bodies of huge organisations, various non-governmental groups and, most importantly, every individual, who, having taken the said path, will always find support. Within their means, each person can strive to expand positive and supportive impact to all the aforementioned areas. Essentially, this message is a spiritual ecology manifesto. Physical contamination of our planet is not as dangerous as the one we are experiencing right now, which has already evoked a drastic punishment and caused millions of people to die in a short period of time. It affects each of us individually and all of us collectively. In the context of this phenomenon, there can be no ambiguities or tolerance to crimes whatsoever.

Safe travels to all of you, who are on the path towards truth and light, in order to protect our planet – home to all of us – and keep its aura (which reflects our communal consciousness) clean and shining brightly. For all nations, families and each and every one of us, this is the only way to survive and live meaningful lives.

Arvydas Daškus

Arvydas Daškus has written a novel "Navigator", collections of poems "The Pyramid" and "Twilight". He is a playwrighter, winner of Motiejus Valančius' Drama Competition. Three of his plays have been staged in the Lithuanian theatres. Two of his drama books „Drama" I and „Drama II" have also been published. In addition, Arvydas Daškus writes ballads and performs them. Despite all of this, this uniquely gifted person is mostly known as a charismatic bioenergetotherapist - healer. As well as being a distinguished practitioner, he is also a theoretician, who has published a series of books called "The Practice of Karma". This is his fifth book in the series. It encompasses the most significant fragments of his previous works and suggests new ways of seeking spiritual development. The author is also known for a unique perspective on the challenging global situation bought by the Covid-19 pandemic.

Viktor Daskus - Technical Lead, Editor, Consultant and General Manager at Cancer Key Lab.